IR

DISCARD

SEP 1 0

Westminster Public Library
3705 W. 112th Ave.
Westminster, CO 80031
www.westminsterlibrary.org

JUMP INTO SPORTS

Soccer

By Bob Temple

Soccer is a fun sport to play. Soccer players kick a ball up and down a long field. They run a lot during a game.

A soccer ball is often black and white.

Soccer players wear shoes with spikes on the bottom. They also wear special pads to **protect** their **shins** from getting kicked.

The spikes on the shoes keep players from slipping on the grass.

A soccer field is a giant rectangle. There is a big **goal** at each end of the field.

A soccer goal has a net to stop the ball.

Each team tries to score by kicking the ball into the other team's goal. They can also bump it into the goal with their heads. But they cannot use their hands!

Some soccer players use their heads to score goals.

Soccer teams have 11 players. One player is the **goalkeeper**. The goalkeeper protects the goal and tries to keep the other team from scoring. Only goalkeepers can use their hands.

Some goalkeepers wear special gloves to help them grip the ball.

The other ten players on each team kick the ball up the field. They pass the ball back and forth with their feet. They try to keep the other team from getting it.

Soccer can be an exciting game to watch.

Defenders play in front of the goalkeeper. They try to keep the other team from kicking toward the goal.

Defenders are also called fullbacks.

Midfielders play in the middle of the field. They help on both **offense** and **defense**.

Midfielders run up and down the field.

Forwards play near the other team's goal. They are sometimes called strikers.

Forwards try to kick the ball into the other team's goal.

When one team gets the ball close to the other team's goal, they take a shot. If it goes in, they score!

It takes teamwork to score a goal.

Glossary

defenders (di-FEND-urz): Defenders are players who play in front of the goalkeeper. Defenders try to stop the other team from scoring.

defense (DEE-fenss): The team that does not have the ball is on defense. The defense tries to get the ball back.

forwards (FOR-wurdz): Forwards are players who play near the other team's goal. The forwards' job is to try to score a goal.

goal (GOHL): A goal is a large frame with a net. In soccer, the players try to kick the ball into the other team's goal.

goalkeeper (GOHL-keep-ur): A goalkeeper is a player who guards his team's goal. A goalkeeper is allowed to use his hands to stop the ball.

midfielders (mid-FEELD-urz): Midfielders are players who play in the middle of the field and run a lot. Midfielders play on both offense and defense.

offense (AW-fenss): The team that has the ball is on offense. The offense tries to score goals.

protect (pruh-TEKT): To protect is to keep something safe from injury. Soccer players wear equipment to protect their legs from getting kicked.

shins (SHINZ): Shins are the lower front part of the leg. Soccer players wear guards to protect their shins.

To Find Out More

Books

Crisfield, Deborah. *The Everything Kids' Soccer Book: Rules, Techniques, and More about Your Favorite Sport!* Avon, MA: Adams Media, 2002.

Falk, Laine. *Let's Talk Soccer.* New York: Children's Press, 2008.

Gifford, Clive. *Soccer: The Ultimate Guide to the Beautiful Game.* New York: Kingfisher Publications, 2002.

Murphy, Patricia J. *Let's Play Soccer.* New York: DK Publishing, 2008.

Web Sites

Visit our Web site for links about soccer:
childsworld.com/links

Note to Parents, Teachers, and Librarians: We routinely verify our Web links to make sure they are safe and active sites. So encourage your readers to check them out!

Index

About the Author

In his long writing career, **Bob Temple** has been a sportswriter and an award-winning author. He has written dozens of books for young readers. Bob owns a development house that specializes in creating children's educational books. He lives with his family in Minnesota.

On the cover: Playing soccer can be a great way to get fit!

Published by The Child's World®
1980 Lookout Drive • Mankato, MN 56003-1705
800-599-READ • www.childsworld.com

ACKNOWLEDGMENTS
The Child's World®: Mary Berendes, Publishing Director
The Design Lab: Design and production
Red Line Editorial: Editorial direction

PHOTO CREDITS: Lewis Wright/iStockphoto, cover; Stefan Klein/iStockphoto, cover; PhotoDisc, 2, 18; iStockphoto, 3; Big Stock Photo, 5, 9, 15, 17, 19; Chris Hill/Shutterstock Images, 7; Mike Flippo/Shutterstock Images, 11; Stuart Hannagan/iStockphoto, 13; Ana Abejon/iStockphoto, 21

Copyright © 2010 by The Child's World®
All rights reserved. No part of this book may be reproduced or utilized in any form or by any means without written permission from the publisher.

Printed in the United States of America in Mankato, Minnesota.
November 2009
F11460

LIBRARY OF CONGRESS CATALOGING-IN-PUBLICATION DATA
Temple, Bob.
  Soccer / by Bob Temple.
    p. cm. — (Jump into sports)
  Includes index.
  ISBN 978-1-60253-372-1 (library bound : alk. paper)
  1. Soccer—Juvenile literature. I. Title. II. Series.
  GV943.25.T44 2010
  796.334—dc22   2009030730

All sports carry a certain amount of risk. To reduce the risk of injury while playing soccer, play at your own level, wear all safety gear, and use care and common sense. The publisher and author take no responsibility or liability for injuries resulting from playing soccer.

Westminster Public Library
3705 W. 112th Ave.
Westminster, CO 80031
www.westminsterlibrary.org